ALIENS

BY JOHN HAMILTON

VISIT US AT

WWW.ABDOPUBLISHING.COM

Published by ABDO Publishing Company, 4940 Viking Drive, Suite 622, Edina, Minnesota 55435.
Copyright ©2007 by Abdo Consulting Group, Inc. International copyrights reserved in all countries.
No part of this book may be reproduced in any form without written permission from the publisher.
ABDO & Daughters™ is a trademark and logo of ABDO Publishing Company.

Printed in the United States.

Editor: Paul Joseph
Graphic Design: John Hamilton
Cover Design: Neil Klinepier
Cover Illustration: *Starsmashers* ©2004 Don Maitz
Interior Photos and Illustrations: p 1 *Starsmashers* ©2004 Don Maitz; p 5 *Triple Detente* ©1986 Don Maitz; p 6 Will Smith in *Men in Black*, Corbis; p 7 *Ratattack* ©1976 Don Maitz; p 8 *Chase into Space* ©1987 Janny Wurts; p 9 alien portrait, Corbis; p 10 alien from *This Island Earth*, Corbis; p 11 *Aliens 10, Humans 3*, ©1977 Don Maitz; p 12 aliens and flying saucer, Corbis; p 13 *Pokerface* ©1976 Don Maitz; p 14 lobby poster for *2001: A Space Odyssey*, courtesy MGM; p 15 Klaatu from *The Day the Earth Stood Still*, Corbis; p 16 scene from *Earth vs. the Flying Saucers*, Corbis; p 17 *Deathworld*, ©2004 Don Maitz; p 18 Martian emerging from spaceship, Corbis; p 19 Martian towering over London, Corbis; p 20 (top) Martian fighting machine, courtesy Paramount Pictures; p 20 (bottom) Tom Cruise in *War of the Worlds*, Corbis; p 21 aliens attack in flying saucers, Corbis; p 22 armada of flying saucers, Corbis; p 23 Ultimate Prize, ©1987 Janny Wurts; p 24 alien from *Predator*, Corbis; p 25 alien queen mother at Science Fiction Museum, Corbis; p 26 scene from *Solaris*, courtesy Twentieth Century Fox; p 27 *E.S.P. Worm*, ©1986 Don Maitz; p 28 SETI radio dish, Corbis; p 29 *The Cavity*, ©1985 Don Maitz; p 31 *Gertrude*, ©1979 Janny Wurts.

Library of Congress Cataloging-in-Publication Data

Hamilton, John, 1959-
   Aliens / John Hamilton.
      p. cm. -- (World of science fiction)
   Includes index.
   ISBN-13: 978-1-59679-986-8
   ISBN-10: 1-59679-986-2
   1. Life on other planets--Juvenile literature. I. Title. II. Series.

QB54.H286 2006
576.8'39--dc22

                           2006002763

CONTENTS

THEY CAME FROM OUTER SPACE

Space Marine Dirk Pontoon gingerly stepped onto the surface of Alpha 21, the rocky planet that had lately caused so much excitement. The hatch of his jump ship closed behind him with a whoosh. Dirk nervously fingered the trigger of his AK-9000 blaster. The ship's computer had told him there were odd life forms on this planet, and Dirk wasn't taking any chances.

Suddenly, Dirk saw it. The creature emerged from the shadows. As it came closer, into the light, Dirk gasped. It was hideous.

Dozens of tentacles writhed and pulsated, sprouting from the middle of a large, bear-sized body. Openings on its frog-like skin oozed slime as the creature slowly dragged its way forward. Two eye-stalks bobbed above the alien's head. Instead of a mouth, there was a gaping hole, and in the hole were rows of sharp and shiny teeth that looked like daggers. The creature unhinged its jaw and let out a terrible screech.

Instinctively, Dirk pulled the blaster trigger. Shoot first and ask questions later, he always said. But… nothing! Jammed again! "Piece of junk," Dirk muttered, as he fumbled for a stun grenade.

Suddenly a high-pitched noise, like a mosquito the size of a bus, filled his head. Dirk put his hands to his ears, but the noise only got worse. It was coming from inside his brain. The creature was communicating with him telepathically! Dirk finally made out the words, spoken in a kind of sing-song melody, like a bird's.

"Hello. Can I help you? Are you lost?"

Facing page: Triple Detente, by Don Maitz.

We are not alone.

Aliens are familiar to anyone who enjoys science fiction. These strange, otherworldly, sometimes bug-eyed creatures are as common in science fiction as detectives in mystery stories, or wizards in fantasy novels. Aliens populate some of our most beloved tales. The characters in *Star Trek* explored strange new worlds and the aliens that inhabited them. The aliens of *Star Wars* included Yoda, Jabba the Hutt, Boba Fett, Chewbacca, and hundreds of others in a galaxy far, far away. In literature, too, aliens are as common as jetpacks and moonbeams, such as the Puppeteers from *Ringworld*, the Overlords from *Childhood's End*, and the Guild Steersmen from *Dune*.

When aliens come to Earth, it can be humbling and wondrous, as in *E.T. the Extraterrestrial*. Or the result can be disastrous. The invading Martians of H. G. Wells's *War of the Worlds* nearly wiped out the entire human race. Sometimes we don't even know when aliens are living among us. In *Men in Black*, government agents kept track of aliens in disguise, hidden from a blissfully ignorant public.

What exactly are aliens? Usually, we think of them as intelligent and sentient, able to have feelings and relate to others and their environment. Some can be good, while others are bad. Some aliens want nothing more than a good meal. They are almost always from a distant planet, although sometimes they live practically next door, on Mars, or even as close as Earth's moon.

Right: Will Smith cuddles an alien baby in *Men in Black*.
Facing page: *Ratattack,* by Don Maitz.

Folklore from cultures worldwide tells of fantastic talking beasts such as dragons or other magical creatures. The myths of ancient Greece and Rome have their all-powerful gods. All of these beings are sentient non-humans. But the aliens of science fiction have something more: they blend human imagination with scientific fact. It's fun to imagine new worlds, and the weird kinds of life that might live there. What might creatures from other planets look like? How would they behave? What would their cultures be like? If an alien planet contained a crushing amount of gravity, would its inhabitants be short and slow-moving? If a planet were airy, would the aliens sprout wings?

Aliens take many, many forms. Some are humanoid, looking much the same as ordinary earthlings. Others are insectoids, like talking cockroaches with large brains. Some are scaly reptilians, while some have no shape at all, like gaseous blobs floating on the breeze.

Movies have dealt with aliens for decades. Authors have written about aliens since before science fiction was a recognized type of literature, or genre. The French author Voltaire wrote *Micromégas* in 1752. The story tells of a pair of giant aliens who visit Earth and mock the puny humans they find there. In 1892, an Australian clergyman named Robert Potter published *The Red Sickness from the Germ Growers*. It may be the first novel about a hostile alien invasion. H. G. Wells's *War of the Worlds* came six years later, in 1898.

Left: A classic alien, with oversized eyes and a large brain. *Facing page: Chase into Space*, by Janny Wurts.

Aliens are often used by authors as a literary device—they are a substitute for examining humankind. In storytelling, aliens can take the place of human beings. They are a way for science fiction authors to talk about controversial issues such as abortion, sexism, or human rights. It's easier to examine tough problems and think about solutions if the problems are happening to an alien society. Aliens can act like a mirror for our own human faults.

One well-known example is Ursula K. Le Guin's *The Left Hand of Darkness*. In the novel, a race of aliens called the Gethenians are much like human beings. They have one trait, though, that is very different—they have the ability to become male some of the time, and female at other times. By reading this story, we begin to think about what it means to be a man or a woman, how prejudiced our views can be, and to see things from different perspectives.

Facing Page: Aliens 10, Humans 3, by Don Maitz. *Below:* An alien from the film, *This Island Earth.*

Space Marine Dirk Pontoon, at the beginning of this chapter, had certain notions about aliens—if they're ugly and have sharp teeth, they must certainly be hostile, right? In a way, isn't that how most of us view people who are different from ourselves? If foreign people don't meet our standards of beauty, or if they dress in strange ways, we look down on them. Worse, we often think they're up to no good. But as Dirk Pontoon discovered, maybe aliens are like the rest of us. Maybe they're just trying to get through the day, or do their chores, or perhaps even help out a stranger in need. Better not be too quick on that trigger finger, space marine.

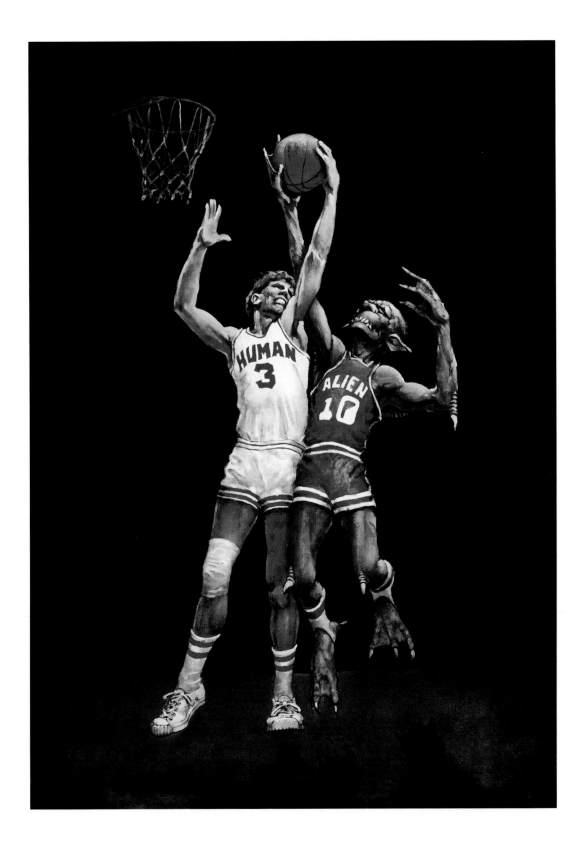

WE COME IN PEACE

In many science fiction stories, first contact between humans and aliens is a wondrous experience, filled with curiosity, perhaps a little suspicion, but much hope for the future. Aliens in these kinds of books and movies are usually an advanced race of beings. They've been watching us a long time, like scientists studying primitive tribes, waiting for mankind to evolve. Are humans ready to join other races in the galaxy, or are we too stupid, or too dangerous, or just not grown up enough?

There is often a test to prove whether mankind is truly ready to join the interstellar community. Humans sometimes fail the test, abandoned alone on Earth to ponder their fate. Other times mankind is deemed worthy by the superior, benevolent aliens. They reward the earthlings with advanced technology or knowledge, beginning a new era of human history.

In Arthur C. Clarke's classic 1953 novel *Childhood's End*, a superior race of aliens called the Overlords helps humanity solve its many problems. Some humans are fearful as they try to guess the aliens' motives. But the Overlords are indeed helpful, and educate human children to the point that they gain superhuman powers.

Right: A group of aliens retreat to their flying saucer.
Facing Page: Pokerface, by Don Maitz.

In Steven Spielberg's 1977 film, *Close Encounters of the Third Kind*, spindly-armed aliens arrive in a huge "mother ship" to take specially selected humans away with them back into space. The reason for the trip is unknown, but for those chosen, the journey promises to be wondrous. The title of the film refers to the final stage of UFO sightings: actual contact with aliens.

In *The Day the Earth Stood Still*, the 1951 thought-provoking film by Robert Wise, humans are tested and found wanting. A superior alien named Klaatu lands in a flying saucer in Washington, D.C. He warns humankind that his alien race will not tolerate the earthlings' development of atomic bombs. Klaatu doesn't particularly care if mankind destroys itself, but if humans threaten other planets with weapons of mass destruction, then Klaatu and his race will annihilate Earth. As a demonstration of power, Klaatu is accompanied by a large, silver-clad robot named Gort, who can melt a tank with a single glance from his heat-ray visor.

Other science fiction tales feature first contact with aliens in more subtle ways. Sometimes contact is like a message left in a bottle, and it's up to the humans to figure out how to take the next step, if they're willing. In director Stanley Kubrick's classic 1968 film, *2001: A Space Odyssey*, written by Kubrick and Arthur C. Clarke, a mysterious slab of stone called a monolith is discovered on the moon. It points to an unknown alien intelligence from an area near the planet Jupiter. Five astronauts are sent in a spaceship to explore the source, and perhaps make contact. Their ship is controlled by a computer called HAL 9000, which is so advanced it may even surpass mankind in intelligence. Things go horribly wrong during the journey, and by the time the ship reaches Jupiter, only one astronaut, David Bowman, is left to confront the aliens. In a mind-bending sequence of events, the alien entity helps Bowman take the next evolutionary leap for humankind.

Facing Page: The alien Klaatu from the film, *The Day the Earth Stood Still. Below:* A lobby poster for the film, *2001: A Space Odyssey.*

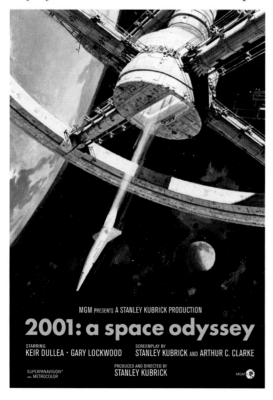

MGM PRESENTS A STANLEY KUBRICK PRODUCTION

2001: a space odyssey

STARRING
KEIR DULLEA · GARY LOCKWOOD

SCREENPLAY BY
STANLEY KUBRICK AND ARTHUR C. CLARKE

SUPERPANAVISION® and METROCOLOR

PRODUCED AND DIRECTED BY
STANLEY KUBRICK

MGM

INVASION!

First contact with aliens doesn't always turn out to be such a nice experience. This is especially true when the aliens are bent on total destruction of our planet! Sometimes, of course, aliens are just trying to survive. They often view humans as a convenient food source. Science fiction is filled with creatures who want nothing more than a tasty human snack.

Some invading aliens are humanoids who look similar to earthlings. They are often depicted with large heads, to better contain the hefty brains that they've evolved. These aliens use their superior intelligence to scheme ways to take over our planet.

Author Damon Knight once wrote an alien-invasion story called, *To Serve Man.* At first, the aliens were nice to humans. They ended war, hunger, and poverty. The reason, they said, was because of a book, which hadn't yet been translated into any human language. The only thing the humans knew was that its title was, *To Serve Man.* Humans were soon invited to the aliens' home planet, and they eagerly lined up like lambs to a slaughter. Only at the end of the story did the hero discover—too late—that the mysterious book was in fact a cookbook. Humans were being sent to the alien planet as the main course in an extraterrestrial feast.

Right: A scene from the 1956 film, *Earth vs. the Flying Saucers.*
Facing page: Deathworld, by Don Maitz.

Other aliens, perhaps not blessed by giant brains, instead use brute force and naked hostility to attack Earth. These are definitely not little green men from Mars! These beasts can be weird and terrifying. They are such a cliché in science fiction that they've been given a nickname: BEM's, which stands for "bug-eyed monsters."

The granddaddy of all alien invasion stories is H.G. Wells's *War of the Worlds,* which was first published as a novel in 1898. For more than 100 years, its influence has made us cast a suspicious eye toward the stars. Are there really aliens up there, watching us, plotting our destruction?

Herbert George Wells (1866-1946) was an important English writer famous for his science-fiction novels. He wrote more than 80 books, including *The Time Machine* in 1895, and *The Invisible Man* in 1897.

In *War of the Worlds,* aliens from Mars flee their dying planet, landing on Earth in giant cylinder-shaped rockets. They begin their invasion by attacking London, England. The Martians use huge "fighting machines," which are pods on top of three long metal legs. Their weapons are "heat rays" and toxic black smoke. The earthlings are helpless against the technologically superior Martians. Victory seems certain for the invaders, but within days they mysteriously begin dropping dead. In one of the great plot twists of science fiction, the Martians become infected by Earth germs, of which they have no natural defense. Humanity is saved by the smallest of creatures.

Facing page: A Martian fighting machine hovers over London, England, from a 1906 edition of *War of the Worlds,* by H. G. Wells. *Below:* A Martian emerges from his spaceship, from a 1906 edition of *War of the Worlds.*

Above: A Martian fighting machine from the 1953 film, *War of the Worlds.*

War of the Worlds was so successful that it spawned many remakes and imitations over the years. On Halloween eve, October 30, 1938, actor Orson Welles and the Mercury Theater produced a radio broadcast version of the story. It featured fake news reports, amazing sound effects, and on-the-spot reporting. Many people believed the broadcast was really happening. As many as one million people panicked, rushing into the streets and fleeing the cities to escape the "alien invasion."

In 1953, Hollywood producer George Pal created a movie version of Wells's book. These modern, updated Martians flew in green manta ray-shaped craft. The machines had weird probes in front, like a cobra's head, which spewed disintegrating death rays. The dizzying visual and sound effects made *War of the Worlds* a movie classic. It won the 1953 Academy Award for best special effects.

Many science fiction novels and movies have imitated the *War of the Worlds* invasion formula. In 1996, Roland Emmerich and Dean Devlin created *Independence Day*, a blockbuster science fiction action movie that featured giant spacecraft, hostile aliens,

death rays, and exploding cities. In the end, mankind's resourcefulness and will to survive finally turned the tide against the invaders.

In 2005, director Steven Spielberg brought yet another version of *War of the Worlds* to movie theaters. Actor Tom Cruise plays a man who must flee New York City with his children as alien invaders begin their reign of destruction. Spielberg included many nods to Wells's original novel, including giant tripod-legged fighting machines and death rays, while keeping a modern and original spin, updating the story for today's audiences.

Left: Tom Cruise in Steven Spielberg's 2005 adaptation of *War of the Worlds.* *Facing page:* Aliens attack!

Tales of alien invasion often reflect our own human fears and concerns. Wells wrote *War of the Worlds* as a way to criticize the English government, which at that time in history was busy invading countries all over the world and making them British colonies.

In the 1950s and early 1960s, people feared the power of the atom. It seemed that the spread of nuclear weapons might easily destroy the world, or the radiation they spread would cause all kinds of horrifying mutations. A rash of giant radiation-caused monsters invaded movie theaters all over the world. Godzilla, Rodan, bug-eyed monsters, even the giant ants from the movie *Them!* were all spawned in a haze of radioactive fear.

Fear also created a slew of invasion movies in which the aliens were hidden among us. The aliens would wait for the right moment to strike, or, without our knowledge, slowly take over our minds and bodies. Many believe that these stories arose because of the Cold War and the "Red Scare," the conflict in the mid-20th century between the democracies of the West, led by the United States, and Communist dictatorships led by China and the Soviet Union. People feared that secret Communist agents were infiltrating high levels of the U.S. government. It was hard to tell who was a friend and who was an enemy. This kind of rampant paranoia was reflected in our popular culture, especially in movies. The most famous example is the 1956 film, *Invasion of the Body Snatchers*, in which a doctor discovers that his town's residents are being replaced by alien duplicates. The movie's producers said it was never intended to be a response to the Cold War, but for many people it reflected perfectly the paranoia that gripped the nation during that time.

Left: An armada of flying saucers speeds toward Earth.
Facing Page: Ultimate Prize, by Janny Wurts.

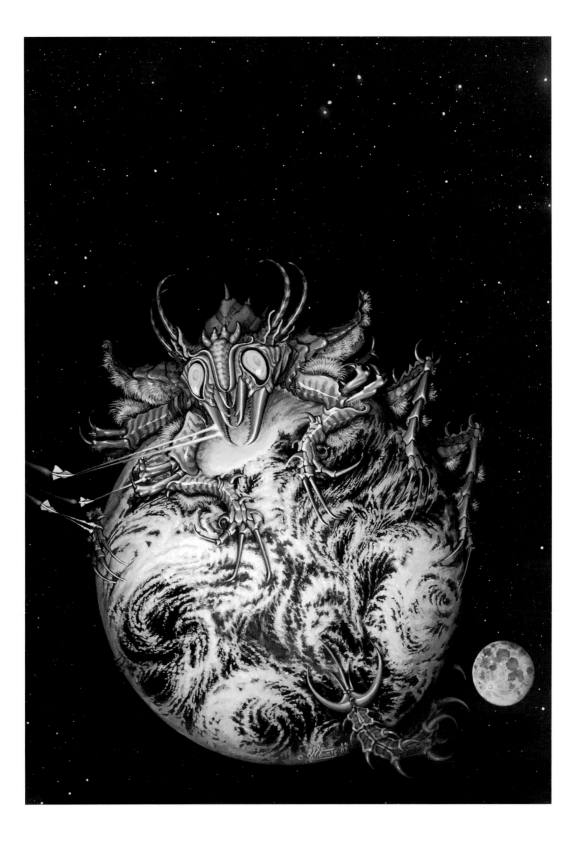

Unidentified Flying Objects (UFOs), rampaging aliens, pod people, and giant radioactive bugs all reflect our fear of invasion and destruction. But sometimes the aliens aren't so easy to spot. Sometimes they're cloaked under clouds of secrecy and government conspiracy. *The X Files* played on that fear quite successfully during its nine seasons on television. FBI agents Fox Mulder and Dana Scully continually uncovered shady plots of alien domination. They fought not only the invaders, but also people in the U.S. government who wanted to keep things secret.

Sometimes aliens can be microscopic, as in Michael Crichton's 1969 sci-fi thriller, *The Andromeda Strain*, which was also made into a movie in 1971. The story revolves around a group of scientists desperately trying to isolate and destroy a deadly virus that has hitchhiked back to Earth aboard a space probe. It's a cautionary tale about military blundering, and how Earth's gravest threat may come not from spaceships and death rays, but from the smallest of organisms, a sort of *War of the Worlds* in reverse.

The Cold War, plus our suspicions of government and new technology, are often used to explain stories of alien conquest. Sometimes, though, a scary alien is simply a substitute for a simple ghost story. Ridley Scott's 1979 film, *Alien*, is often described as a haunted house story set in outer space. The creatures in *Alien*, as well as its sequels, are some of the most imaginative and horrifying ever created.

Right: A worker at the Science Fiction Museum in Seattle, Washington, prepares an exhibit of an 18-foot (5.5-m) Alien Queen Mother from the movie *Aliens*. *Facing Page:* An alien from the 1987 film, *Predator*.

BEYOND OUR COMPREHENSION

In many science fiction stories, aliens prove too bizarre, or different from humans, for us to even comprehend them. They truly are "alien," so much so that it's difficult to detect their existence. In Fritz Leiber's 1964 novel, *The Wanderer*, a mysterious artificial planet suddenly appears out of hyperspace into Earth's orbit. Earth's moon is torn apart, and humans are faced with earthquakes, tsunamis, and other calamities caused by the Wanderer's massive gravitational pull. An alien presence guides the Wanderer, but the god-like visitors are completely indifferent to mankind's plight, as if the humans were mere insects. All the humans can do is hang on and try to survive.

In Polish author Stanislaw Lem's *Solaris*, published in 1961, an entire ocean planet is an alien life form. When an astronaut arrives to study the new world, he is confronted by the physical likeness of his dead wife. The ghostly vision is apparently fueled by the astronaut's painful memories of her. The scientist learns that others are also experiencing these disturbing visions. He comes to the conclusion that the planet itself may be some kind of massive brain that is using the humans' memories to make contact. But why? And how can we ever understand our complex universe when we make so many assumptions about consciousness, intelligence, and life itself?

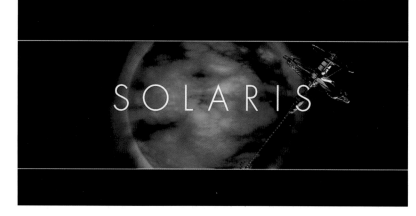

Right: A scene from the 2002 Steven Soderbergh film, *Solaris.*
Far Right: E.S.P. Worm, by Don Maitz.

REAL ALIENS?

Could there really be aliens out there among the stars? Is it possible they may someday visit Earth? There's no scientific evidence that proves alien life. But many scientists and astronomers believe there's a good chance that life exists on other worlds. The universe holds many trillions of stars. The odds are good that some of these harbor the right conditions for life, which most scientists say include liquid water and temperatures similar to Earth. Alien life may resemble simple bacteria, advanced civilizations capable of space travel, or something so bizarre that we don't even recognize it as a life form.

If aliens do exist on other planets, why haven't they made themselves known to us? Some believe that aliens have already made contact. As proof, they point to the many UFO sightings made over the last century. They believe governments and the military hide the existence of aliens in order to protect human populations, which might panic at the knowledge that we are not alone.

A more likely reason, however, is that aliens haven't discovered our little out-of-the-way planet just yet. Most people don't realize just how big our universe really is. Our galaxy alone, the Milky Way, is so immense that it takes light 100,000 years just to cross from one end to the other. It contains more than 100 billion stars. And the distance between the stars is incredibly vast. Finding Earth would be harder than finding a needle in a haystack.

Some believe the most practical way to make alien contact is by monitoring radio waves. The SETI Project (SETI

Below: SETI Project radio dishes monitor space, searching for signs of extraterrestrial life.

stands for "Search for Extra-Terrestrial Intelligence") began in the 1960s with the goal of searching for intelligent life in other parts of our galaxy. The SETI Project scans deep space with huge telescopes that detect radio waves, searching for possible alien signals. It's not an easy task. Space is huge, and there are many radio frequencies to search. Even after many years of listening, with help from the most advanced computers available, nothing yet has been detected. But the hunt continues. If an alien signal finally reaches Earth, it will answer a question that has haunted mankind for thousands of years: are we alone? Is there anybody else out there?

Left: The Cavity, by Don Maitz.

GLOSSARY

BEM

A word sometimes used in science fiction stories, which stands for "bug-eyed monsters."

Cold War

The mainly diplomatic conflict waged between the United States and the former Soviet Union after World War II. The Cold War resulted in a large buildup of weapons and troops. It ended when the Soviet Union broke up in the late 1980s and early 1990s.

Earthling

An inhabitant of the planet Earth. In science fiction, an alien might call a human being an earthling.

Extraterrestrial

Something that comes from outside the earth or its atmosphere. In most science fiction stories, an extraterrestrial is a sentient alien from another planet.

Galaxy

A system of millions, or even hundreds of billions, of stars and planets, clustered together in a distinct shape, like a spiral or ellipse. Earth is located within the Milky Way Galaxy.

Genre

A type, or kind, or a work of art. In literature, a genre is distinguished by a common subject, theme, or style. Some genres include science fiction, fantasy, and mystery.

Humanoid

Looking like or behaving like a human being. A humanoid alien would typically have a torso, four limbs, and a head.

Hyperspace

A kind of space that exists in theory (and in many science fiction stories), in which a craft can travel faster than the speed of light.

INTERSTELLAR

Something that happens or exists between the stars of a galaxy. A rocketship that travels through interstellar space is moving from one star system to the next.

PARANOIA

A fear, or suspicion, of people or their actions, even when there's no direct evidence of harm. In the mid-20th century, many Americans had a paranoia about Communist countries, such as the former Soviet Union and China. This fear showed up in the kinds of movies people liked to watch, especially science fiction films about sneaky invading aliens. A good example is *Invasion of the Body Snatchers*.

SENTIENT

Able to have feelings, or sense feelings in others. It can also mean simply being conscious, with an awareness of the outside world. For example, in science fiction, a sentient alien would be able to communicate with humans from Earth, or at least be aware of their presence. A simple microbe, or germ, from another planet would not be sentient (unless it's a very special microbe beyond our current understanding of what defines "life" and "consciousness").

SETI PROJECT

A system of large telescopes and receiver dishes that monitors radio waves in the search for extraterrestrial life. SETI stands for "Search for Extra-Terrestrial Intelligence."

UFO

An Unidentified Flying Object. In science fiction, a UFO is typically some kind of alien craft, such as a flying saucer.

Right: Gertrude, by Janny Wurts.

INDEX